Introduction

This book contains proven steps and strategies on how to make substantial amounts of money out of stocks worth pennies each.

Have you ever wondered whether you could play the stock market game like the experts? This book will prove that you most definitely can. You don't have to be a millionaire to do this. You'll just need a few bucks, an internet connection, and a love of learning to start your journey into continuous wealth.

Thanks again for downloading this book, I hope you enjoy it!

Introducing Penny Stocks

Buying a share of stock from a company makes you the owner of a portion of that company's earnings and assets. The company will then use the money they get from shareholders like you to fund their business. When they make profits, you will also get some of it since you're considered as a partial owner. Thus, stocks benefit both companies and investors and the practice of buying stocks have persisted until this day.

Penny stocks are usually defined as stocks that are sold at one dollar or less. The Securities and Exchange Commission has assigned a $5 or less value to them. Values assigned to penny stocks may differ among individuals, but the common characteristic is that they are the cheapest kind of stocks around. They can even cost one cent each, hence the name penny stocks.

Penny stock companies are usually those that have a market capitalization of less than 100 million dollars. Market capitalization is the total value of a company's stock shares, which is computed by multiplying the number of stocks sold by the price of each stock. Penny stock companies have relatively less market capitalization compared to blue chip (expensive and high quality) companies, which can have billions of dollars' worth of shares.

Explaining The Existence of Penny Stocks

Companies that sell penny stocks are usually small ones that are just beginning their operations. They haven't generated much wealth yet so they are willing to sell their stocks to the public at a very low price. This will hopefully encourage buyers to invest in the company so that there will be enough money to accomplish things.

Companies use penny stocks to do the following:

- **To make up for lack of finances.** It's difficult for starting companies to borrow money from banks and other traditional lenders because they haven't proven their credibility yet. Stocks function as their financial net during these initial stages, but they shouldn't be dependent on their stocks alone all the time.

- **To fund developments.** A company may decide to make improvements, such as purchasing new equipment, renting new buildings, hiring more personnel, enhancing their operations, and advertising to a broader audience. These entail additional costs that they may not be able to pay for with their current level of revenue. In the meantime, they can get the needed support from their penny stock investors.

- **To solve problems.** A company may run into problems like lawsuits, equipment breakdowns, employee drains, etc. Money from stocks will help address these issues when internal resources are scarce.

- **To be more visible.** Aside from acting as a company's financial support, penny stocks also serve as advertisements. When people buy stocks from a company, a trusting relationship is formed. It's possible that the stockholders will offer other kinds of assistance because of this. Cash generated from penny stocks can also pay for continuing their inclusion in stock market listings, which makes them more visible to investors and other beneficial people.

Here are some ways that companies misuse penny stocks. When you discover that a company is doing these activities, think twice about buying or keeping shares from them. Doing so may put your stocks at risk.

- **To get money for personal use.** There are corrupt people in companies who will use income from stocks for their own instead of letting it sustain the business. You have to investigate the credibility of the company's management team; be wary of those with a history of swindling.

- **To keep the company from going bankrupt.** When the business isn't making progress, the only thing that may be keeping them around are investors' contributions. Be careful! When these also run out, there will be nothing left for anyone. This is why it's vital to get accurate and updated insights about the company's earning capabilities.

The Benefits of Investing in Penny Stocks

The following characteristics of penny stocks make them an attractive investment option:

- **Affordability.** Penny stocks are hands-down the cheapest kind of stocks available. If you don't have heaps of money to use for investing in something, consider starting out with penny stocks. Their low prices will allow you to spread your investments by buying stocks from many companies. That way, you will have many sources of passive income and you will avoid losing all your money in case you invested completely in a failed company.

- **Chance of earning huge dividends.** Did you know that big companies today were once selling penny stocks? American Airlines, Concur Technologies, Ford, Monster Beverages, Nokia, and True Religion were once fledgling companies that have stocks worth pennies each. They have made it big over the years with good business practices and sheer determination. Their shareholders also got rich without really doing anything but invest in the right companies at the right time.

- **Fast earnings.** A special characteristic of stocks is that their value can change within a matter of hours. You can buy penny stocks, monitor its value, and sell them when they hit a peak rate. You don't have to wait years for this to happen; you can get profits from your investments within the week or even within the day, if you're really lucky.

The Disadvantages of Penny Stocks

Buying penny stocks is similar to taking a gamble because you're buying something that may or may not provide you profits in the future. Acquiring penny stocks is riskier than getting blue chip stocks because they come from companies that are not that stable yet. There is a chance that their businesses will fail and when they do, their stocks will also decrease in value or even reach zero. If that happens, you will incur a loss in your investment. You may be forced to sell your stocks before their values plummet even further, or hang around and wait until the tides change.

These are the reasons why penny stocks companies and their stocks are not as reliable as established ones:

- **Limitations in resources.** Penny stocks companies are relying on a few assets and if something happens to these few items, it's easy to derail the entire system. Compare this situation to large companies; they have a lot to work with so a few losses will not matter much. Companies' resources also include the individuals who serve, manage and protect the business. It's easy for them to be lured away by prestigious companies because they are promised higher salaries and other perks. Unfortunately, without them, the company falls apart and their stocks go with it.

- **Few investors.** Since penny stocks companies are new to the market, it's most likely that they haven't made their presence felt yet and they have attracted only a few investors. Thus, these companies may not get enough money to perform well. Also, when only a handful of people are investing in a company, it's possible that the company's market capitalization value will decrease significantly when some of them back out. This is especially true when these investors are contributing to crucial processes in that company.

- **Fraud.** Unscrupulous individuals sometimes take advantage of people's lack of knowledge about penny companies. They will dupe them into thinking that they're good investments even though their worth is close to none. They may encourage buyers by giving them talks and publications about how the company will make them earn a lot of cash. They can even go as far as provide fake reports and statistics about the company's performance. This will cause the shareholders to willingly hand over their cash to these people, who may then run off with their money when the company becomes bankrupt.

- **Low popularity.** When people are clueless about the companies you're investing in, they might not be willing to trade or buy stocks from you. The government may likewise be unfamiliar with these companies, so they may not provide these companies with what they need to combat fraud.

Making Penny Stocks Work

As with any kind of stocks, penny stocks have a risk attached to them. To beat your losses, this is what you should do:

- Research companies thoroughly

- Pick only the top performers

- Assess situations carefully

- Maximize your gains and minimize your losses

These steps will be discussed further in the next chapters.

Opening A Brokerage Account

To handle penny stocks, you need to have a brokerage account or a broker. Trading penny stocks used to be done in person with a broker or by talking to one over the phone. Nowadays, trading stocks are done over the Internet and brokers have taken their services online as well.

You need to find a legitimate website where you can buy and sell penny stocks - searching for online brokerage websites or penny stocks trading websites will give you a couple of links along with reviews.

Choose a site that provides you with substantial information about stocks such as price trackers, graphs, charts, reports, etc. Check whether the site has real-time data streams; you need to have updated info because stock prices sometimes fluctuate rapidly.

When you find a legal, comprehensive, and updated brokerage site, register for an account. Remember your account details and set a username and password that's hard for hackers to guess. When you're logging on to your account from computers that are not your own, make sure that you completely log off to prevent strangers from messing with your stocks and possibly withdrawing your money into their own account.

These criteria will help you select the best brokerage sites:

- **Trading options.** The brokerage and the broker must allow you to trade penny stocks. Some concentrate on high-end stocks only; these are useless for penny stocks trading. Other than this, find out if a brokerage sets restrictions on the markets you can trade with.

- **How much it costs for you to create an account.** Getting an account costs only $20 or less. Just make sure that you join in a quality site.

- **Charges for penny stock trades.** You are charged a percentage of how much your stock is worth. The rate for commission may vary among differently priced shares. For penny stocks, go with the brokerages with the lowest commission rates.

- **Rules for maintaining the account.** Read the rules, terms and conditions, and instructions of the site. There are websites that penalize account users that don't comply with rules or forget payments.

- **User-friendliness.** Try different online brokerage sites to see whether you'll be comfortable in using them. Registering for an account that you can't use is a waste of your money.

- **Data availability and presentation.** Many penny stocks trading sites offer tools to analyze stocks data and they are presented in a format that makes you easily see how these stocks are faring. You can get some information for free from finance websites, but you may have to pay extra for additional analytical tools.

- **Speed of transactions.** Trading stock can take place within minutes, or it can take up to a few days. Keep in mind that what you do in the online account may not immediately reflect the actual status of the stocks. Know the specific duration of how long a transaction takes effect and double check the progress with a real-life broker.

- **Customer service.** A reliable site allows you to contact the people behind the brokerage account. Test whether the hotlines work and ask more information about the site from the service crew.

After registering for an account, you will have to provide your bank or checking account to the brokerage website and connect it. Linking may take a few minutes or up to days depending on the site or the bank. When the account is validated, send money to your brokerage account to complete your application and to work with stocks. Prepare for a possible days-long delay before you can start using your account. To avoid inconveniences, read the site's manual to know how long it takes for processes and transactions to be completed and prepare accordingly.

You will have access to the following tools once you are logged in:

- **A graphical depiction of stock prices.** This will let you know how much your stock is worth. You can also track price changes throughout time.

- **Comparisons between different stocks.** You can choose what penny stocks you want to compare amongst alternatives. There are filter options such as company types, industries, etc. Use this tool to get the top picks and to eliminate the poor performers in a group.

- **A tool that enables you to trade stocks.** It's similar to purchasing or selling from an online shop. You click on the stock and you specify details such as the price, number of stocks you intend to buy or sell, and so on. Make sure that you set limits on the number of stocks you intend to deal with. This will make you give your own specifications that are based on your research and analysis of the data you have gathered from different sources. There are options that make you sell or buy stocks in bulk from different penny stock companies, which may have varying prices for stocks each. If you can control the details of the transaction, there's a better chance that you will gain more than you lose.

- **A tool that allows communication with a real life broker.** Talking with a human broker is important because a program can only do so much. Feel free to contact your broker to know whether handling a stock from a company is a good idea or not, or whenever you are having problems with your stocks.

Investment Strategies

Understanding how penny stocks work and knowing how you can get your hands on them are not enough to make you successful in penny stocks investments. You also have to learn how to use them the right way.

Investment Tips

- **Set your investment goals.** Putting your objectives clearly will help you in making investment decisions. Penny stock values can fluctuate and you might get distracted by other investment options. Sticking with your plans will help you accomplish what you really want. It will put your focus on things you really have to pay attention to, such as stock market trends, company performances, etc.

- **Plan your investments.** When you have enumerated your penny stocks investment goals, set plans on how you can achieve them. Include specific action plans such as how you're going to research about your stocks, when you'll talk with company representatives, the specific signs that will tell you when to sell your stocks, and the like. Also, set Plan Bs and Plan Cs to make you cope just in case your main plan doesn't work.

- **Diversify your investments.** Investing your cash on penny stocks means taking chances to gain money, to lose money, or be stuck where you started. When you buy from varying kinds of companies, you may save yourself from losses just in case an industry becomes beset with problems. It will also give you multiple sources of income. You may also try other types of investments other than penny stocks; you might benefit from them as well for as long as you can manage your penny stocks.

Methods to Get the Best Companies to Invest In

- **Stock market research**. You can consult stock market information and study how a stock behaves over time to predict whether it will yield substantial profits in the future.

- **Company research.** If you are focusing on a particular company, spend time in investigating how well they are doing. Things to know are their sales, profit, debt, and the like. This will give you an insight in their potential and their capability of growing your investment.

- **Comparison with other companies.** A practical way of getting a higher chance of making profits from stocks is to study how companies are faring and to invest in only the top performing companies.

Choosing A Penny Stock Company

The quality of stocks you get are highly dependent on the performance of the company it represents. The best companies to choose are those with the following characteristics:

Reliable Management. If you can, know about the structure of the company and the people that compose each team. Find out about their backgrounds. Search for their names online and see whether you can derive information about their accomplishments and personalities. When you come across someone with a bad reputation or a history of cheating or business mismanagement, it's a practical choice to look for another company. You can talk to these people and request for an interview to have a better feel of what they are like. You can also get in touch with individuals who know them or have worked for them.

Little Debt. Finance sites can offer free information on the debt status of companies. You can also gather valuable company-provided data on the stock exchange markets. From there, you'll find financial reports about the company's assets, liabilities, earnings, and so on. Don't forget to check how much their liabilities are worth. If the company hasn't submitted their report yet (which is required in SEC registered markets), search for news about the company and see whether they have incurred debt. However, don't let a small amount of debt convince you that a company is a good choice. They should be able to do something to erase the debt as time goes by. If you check the company reports after a few months and you see that it's still there, this will alert you that they're not doing something to solve it and they might be neglecting other important business necessities as well.

Many Sources of Income. Consult the company report and see whether the company has acquired many ways to generate income. If this is not available, check news sources. If the company has made significant progress, news about it will surface in the papers or online. You may visit their websites or consult representatives to learn about how they're getting money into the company. Take note of dubious schemes of getting money, such as illegal pyramiding schemes, promoting their company falsely, or promising high interest rates on investments. These financial structures may collapse and they might land into legal trouble, which will greatly diminish or completely negate the worth of their stocks.

Increasing Popularity. When you notice that the company is sending ripples through the market and they are getting listed in more stock exchange markets, it is a sign that they have generated enough money to make themselves more visible. Aside from that, the increased popularity also tends to attract more investors, which boosts their net worth and stock values. Keep an eye on companies with catchy advertisements, attractive logos, and memorable names. People are easily swayed by good advertising, so if a company catches the market's attention, it's very likely that more will buy from them, and the richer the company will get.

Customer Retention. The progress report includes how many clients they have gained and retained. Root for the companies that retain a significant percentage of their gained clients. The number of customers that a company has will have an impact to its wealth and stock value. You can even calculate how much a stock will increase according to this percentage. For example, if a company has gained a 3% increase in customers, you can estimate your stocks to reflect a similar raise as well. When you notice that a company's client base is gradually declining, it is fair to say that the quality of the company may be deteriorating. This will also make investors lose their interest, and when they do, you can expect that the selling price of the stocks will also flop.

Increasing Demand. When more people are clamoring for the company's products or services, it makes prices go up and therefore increases the company's income. Pay attention to how people react to the company. The best companies to choose are those that offer things that nobody else can provide but them. This will make buyers be willing to pay extra because of the rarity of the goods and the necessity of buying from them. When you observe that people are not interested, drop the stocks. A low demand means there are less or no money flowing into the company.

Company Growth. Compare the old reports of the company with the more recent ones. Are they improving at a steady state? Are they earning a lot more, or are their revenues dwindling? Improvement of the company's conditions translates into higher selling prices of stocks. Good online brokerage sites will let you see increases of stock prices. These are the stocks that are more likely to yield a profit for you.

Few Competitors. Research the market and find similar companies to your target company. Are they competing with each other? Or is a company the only one like it in your area? Few competitors mean that there is more demand for the company, and as the demand increases, so is the value assigned to that company. You can use the online tool filter to group similar companies together in a single presentation. Compare how well they rate against each other. However, take note that online sites can have limited company selections. You have the responsibility to keep yourself updated of new rival companies that are cropping up.

Growth Spurts. The best companies to choose are those that have many factors pointing out to its rapid progress. Just make sure that there is real evidence that the company is doing well instead of fake stories about its achievements. You may refer to independent analysts, objective news sources, and third-party investigations of companies.

Selling substantial amount of stocks. When you see that the company is selling more stocks in a regulated stock market, this will tell you that the company currently has a lot of money to spend for the listing. It also brings more money in the company so the value of their stocks will also shoot up.

Narrowing Down The Choices

To make your choice easier, you can narrow down your picks according to the following criteria:

Familiarity. If you're knowledgeable about a particular field like automotive, medicine, or agriculture, it may be best for you to choose a company that functions within that arena. Your understanding of what goes on in the industry will give you a better evaluation of how a company is expected to perform within the present situations.

Higher Stock Prices. Penny stocks can cost anywhere from a cent to 5 dollars. If you limit yourself to stocks priced at the higher end of this range, you are more likely to get stocks from higher quality companies.

Trading Patterns. Tools for analyzing stocks will make you see whether a particular company is currently selling its stocks and for how much. If you notice that a stock has become inactive, it's possible that the listing has ended. If so, it can either mean that they have stopped making stocks available for the public or that they can no longer afford to pay for the listings. In either case, these stocks may not be valid anymore. Analyzing the patterns of stock activity using your common sense and intuition will also give you an idea of whether the stock will increase or decrease in value.

Company Characteristics. Research about the qualities of good companies and then apply this to your stock market selection. You may choose a company of a certain size, revenue, or number of stocks available. By setting standards, you narrow down your options and focus on what may give you the best returns.

Avoiding Dangers in Investing Penny Stocks

Do not rely solely on friends and family's advice about stocks. People often make this common mistake of trusting somebody's information just because they are close to them. Instead, research your stock objectively.

Similarly, do not trust people who come to you out of the blue and talk about stocks. They may hand you some leaflets promoting the company. They may goad you with success stories or promises. Be careful because the facts and narrations provided there may not be truthful. As always, do your own research.

Find out everything you can about the company and their stocks. Use only reliable sources of information that are backed up by evidence. There are instances when criminals have fooled people with fabricated data about company stocks. They have lured buyers with exaggerated figures and manipulated them to purchase the company's stocks. In most cases, a lot of investors were involved and the sudden demand greatly increased the perceived value of the stocks. The fraudsters then sold these stocks to others while the price was still high, but later on, everyone discovered that there is no real value behind the stocks. Unfortunately, the stocks have already been sold by the tricksters and the people who currently own the stocks were left empty handed. Don't let this happen to you by doing thorough investigations and consulting reliable sources of information.

Only trade penny stocks in official markets such as Nasdaq, OTC-BB, and AMEX. These screen companies who apply for listing and they require a regular payment to continue their participation. This will ensure that you get well-performing penny stock companies that have steadily earned money to allow their continued payments to stock listings. Also, these markets have securities in place to deter fraudsters from entering the scene. Stay away from dubious markets that are not monitored by the proper authorities. For example, casual meetings with people for selling or buying penny stocks, or browsing the pink sheets, which any company can use without providing details about their financial and operational status. If you're not sure about the legitimacy of a stock market exchange, you may inquire at the Securities and Exchange Commission about them.

Stay with stable penny stocks companies only. There are people who choose underperforming stocks because they think that these will suddenly improve once the company settles things. This is an error of judgment; stocks do not balance themselves into periods of decline and growth. It's better to analyze the actual conditions of the company before committing to their shares.

Considering The Effects of Special Cases

There are particular situations that have effects on stocks. Here are some of them:

Mergers

When a company merges with another, the cost of their stocks are affected. Generally, when you have stocks of the company that's about to be absorbed, they may be bought from you by the larger company that wants to incorporate the smaller company into itself. You may be paid higher than what you have originally paid so it's a good time to sell. If you decide to hold on to your stocks, it's possible that its value will decrease especially if it gets completely merged to the other company. Also, you may have no choice but to sell anyway when the company entirely loses its identity, and you might be selling at a loss. However, the merger may be discontinued and your company may thrive, so there's a slim chance that you'll profit in the end.

If your company is the one doing the absorbing and it has successfully meshed with another company, expect that the cost of your stocks will jump higher. The resources of the other company will be pooled with your invested company, which enhances its value. However, it's not usual for penny stocks companies to do this because they are usually in the early stages and they have neither experience nor cash to buy other companies to make them their own.

When companies cooperate, they may share their stocks amongst each other. This may mean that there will be a higher number of stocks available. They might either increase or decrease the value of the stocks depending on their target. Whenever you get news about mergers, know what they plan to do with their stocks. If they plan to increase, consider selling them when they do increase. If the prices are set to decrease, try to sell them to others at the current price before costs run down.

Bankruptcy

Bankruptcy is not good for penny stocks. When you invest in a company that is about to run out or is already done for, you won't get anything out of the stocks you bought from them. It may be impossible for you to sell them to other investors. If left with no choice, you can just hope that the company picks itself up again. When they do, your shares may regain their value. But remember, when a business has failed, it's very hard for it to restart. It's better to avoid investing in failing companies in the first place rather than hope for the best after the well runs dry. Always keep your ears open for news about the real financial status of companies. Avoid buying stocks without researching first because they might be from bankrupt companies that are made to look like they're still thriving.

Lawsuits

One thing that online analytical tools may not pick up are the lawsuits filed upon a company. Larger companies may get away unscathed by legal action filed against them, especially if they have an excellent legal and management team who are capable of winning such lawsuits. However, smaller penny stock companies may be in trouble especially because they have little money to deal with such issues. When you spot a company that seems to do incredibly well, do not forget to check whether someone has filed a suit against them. There's a possibility that they might lose the case. The worst-case scenario is that they are forced to stop their operations entirely. If they do, you'll lose everything you have paid for the company's stocks.

How To Improve Your Penny Stock Skills

Stock market trading is hard even if it involves very inexpensive penny stocks. You can lose big if you chose the wrong stock; more especially if you bought a large quantity of it. One thing you can do to minimize your potential errors is to practice with virtual stock market trading first. Find sites that offer paper trading or virtual trading for penny stocks. You don't have to pay anything for acquiring stocks but you don't get to earn from them either. You simply gain the experience of working with stocks minus actual cash.

Whether or not you are using actual cash-based stocks or paper stocks, it's best if you record your endeavors. Brokerage sites may offer this function, but if not, writing notes will do. A notebook can contain notes about companies such as news clippings, promotional material, financial reports, and everything that gives you a view of what their actual worth is or will be. Track their activities and see how it corresponds to changes in their stock values. When you get the hang of investigating company efforts, outside conditions, and their reflections on the stock market, you may enhance your estimating abilities about how their stocks will fare in the future. Use this insight in deciding what to do with the stock.

Always remember: the stock market is not totally predictable via calculations so don't be confined to analysis and projections. Some investors rely on non-analytical skills such as hunches in making their investment decisions. If you are into trying alternative ways of thinking, try learning how to develop your intuitive insights. These will complement the data you gathered and the analysis you make. However, take note that intuition doesn't do all the work for you. It will only supply you with a bigger picture that you might have missed by concentrating on details and limited information too closely.

Learn from your mistakes. The cleverest investors have experienced great losses in penny stock trading but that didn't stop them from trying harder. Like you, they have learned methods to weed out the good companies from the bad, and they have developed their talents of tracking stock patterns and knowing whether it's the right time to buy or sell. Whenever you commit errors, write them down on your journal. This will make sure that you don't forget what occurred and you can avoid doing them again.

Whether you win or lose cash, you still gain in experience. Let each action you take empower you into making better choices. If you stick with it, you may get boundless wealth from something as little as stocks that are worth only pennies.

Conclusion

Thank you again for downloading this book!

I hope this book was able to help you to gain knowledge and confidence to pursue penny stock investments in the stock market.

The next step is to go out there and play!

Finally, if you enjoyed this book, then I'd like to ask you for a favor, would you be kind enough to leave a review for this book on Amazon? It'd be greatly appreciated!

Thank you and good luck!

Printed in France by Amazon
Brétigny-sur-Orge, FR

20858316R00016